BIRD
PAINTINGS

BIRD PAINTINGS

NORMAN ARLOTT
S.W.L.A.

WORLD'S WORK LTD

For Marie, Lisa, Mark and Donna

Copyright © 1982 by Norman Arlott
Published by World's Work Ltd
The Windmill Press, Kingswood, Tadworth, Surrey
Reproduced and printed in Great Britain by Mullis Morgan Ltd

ISBN 0 437 00630 1

Acknowledgements

I would like to thank here the persons that made possible many things that seemed impossible.

Mr John G. Williams who made my visits to Kenya possible, and whilst I was there gave me much help and encouragement and a great deal of his unique knowledge of African birds.

Mr Roger A. Caras for making possible my visit to the U.S.A. and for his kind hospitality during my stay.

Mr Stefan Graham who introduced me to many of the U.S.A.'s birds during our travels in Maryland and Virginia.

Mr and Mrs Sandy Mactaggart who not only gave me and my family full range on their Scottish island estate but also made other things possible.

There are of course many other people who have allowed me, in one way or another, to gather special knowledge, but I owe a special thank you to:
Mr Jack Block, Mr Robert Gillmor, Mr Eric Hosking, Mr Basil Parsons and Mr Andrew Williams.

Lastly and by no means least, I must thank my wife Marie, without whose constructive comments I would accomplish much less.

The Birds

GANNET *Sula bassana*
Most coastal areas in Europe and eastern North America

LITTLE EGRET *Egretta garzetta*
Occurs in many of the warmer parts of Europe as well as Africa, the Middle East and Asia

LOUISIANA HERON *Egretta tricolor*
Coastal areas of eastern and southern U.S.A.

WHITE-FACED TREE DUCK *Dendrocygna viduata*
Locally throughout Africa south of the Sahara

AMERICAN WOOD DUCK *Aix sponsa* Adult male
Eastern U.S.A.

AMERICAN KESTREL *Falco sparverius* Adult male
U.S.A. and Canada

BLACK-WINGED STILT *Himantopus himantopus*
Africa and Asia, the Middle East and many places in the warmer parts of Europe

LITTLE RINGED PLOVER *Charadrius dubius*
Europe

BARN OWL *Tyto alba*
Nearly world wide, temperate and tropical

TURTLE DOVE *Streptopelia turtur*
Europe, wintering in south of range and Africa

KINGFISHER *Alcedo atthis*
Europe

GREY-HEADED KINGFISHER *Halcyon leucocephala*
East and central Africa

WHITE-THROATED BEE-EATER *Merops albicollis*
Africa, south of the Sahara

GREAT SPOTTED WOODPECKER *Dendrocopos major* Adult male
Europe

PIED WAGTAIL *Motacilla alba yarrellii* Adult male
British race of the common European White wagtail

WREN *Troglodytes troglodytes*
Europe

TUFTED TIT *Parus bicolor*
Eastern North America

BEARDED REEDLING *Panurus biarmicus* Two adult males
Patchy European distribution

FAIRY BLUE FLYCATCHER *Erannornis longicauda*
East Africa

REDSTART *Phoenicurus phoenicurus* Adult male
Europe, wintering south to Africa

WHEATEAR *Oenanthe oenanthe* Adult male
Europe, wintering south to Africa

SCARLET-CHESTED SUNBIRD *Nectarinia senegalensis* Adult male
East and central Africa

RUBY-CROWNED KINGLET *Regulus calendula* Adult male
North America

NORTHERN CARDINAL *Cardinalis cardinalis* Adult male
Eastern and southern U.S.A.

BULLFINCH *Pyrrhula pyrrhula* Adult male
Europe

AMERICAN GOLDFINCH *Carduelis tristis* Two adult males and an adult female
North America

YELLOW-CROWNED BISHOP *Euplectes afer* Adult male
East and central Africa

BLUE JAY *Cyanocitta cristata*
North America

*For identification the name of each bird is printed on the reverse of the plates

Introduction

When I was first invited to produce the paintings for this book it was suggested that I portray my twenty-eight favourite birds — on the face of it that seemed a straightforward task until I tried selecting the birds to be featured. It became clear that I did not have many particular favourites. I had favourite families, the chats, bee-eaters and kingfishers sprang immediately to mind, hence the Wheatear and Redstart, and the two kingfishers, the European and the African Grey-headed. Apart from these I considered my favourite birds to be those that I happen to be watching at any given time, be they the ubiquitous House sparrow or Blackbird in my garden or the more exotic birds of the African bush.

As selecting the birds did not seem to work, I turned to the places I had visited, from the local disused gravel pits to the Kakemega forest in Kenya, the Isle of Islay to New York's Long Island. Although not wishing to put birds in landscapes of these areas, little cameos that I had sketched or remembered on such visits appeared to be ideal — the many memory paintings I had stored over the years but had never put on paper, here was my opportunity.

These cameos flooded my mind: the elegant Louisiana heron that strode along the edge of an inlet during the early evening at a Maryland wildfowl refuge, a Gannet battling with the wind during a stormy morning off the Isle of Islay and the well named Scarlet-chested sunbird feeding incessantly among the flowers of an Erythrina. Although on these particular paintings the birds were a prime factor of my attention, in many of the others the birds that appear are there for no other reason than their being in situ while I was more involved in some other aspect of the birds' habitat. There was, for example, the Ruby-crowned kinglet that sought shelter beneath oak leaves in a Long Island copse as I was noting how the rain water ran off the tree branches and leaves. And there was the Turtle dove that sat unnoticed, as I sketched the flowers of its chosen perch, a Horse chestnut, until a slight movement gave its presence away — the flowers and the dove a perfect combination for an English summer day.

I have tried in many of these paintings to produce not just bird portraits but paintings that hopefully show some mood or habitat niche that is an integral part of the bird's world. The original invitation to produce these paintings did, therefore, not only give me the pleasure of painting birds but also of reliving many happy memories from my field trips in Britain and America and my number one bird area, East Africa. I hope that I have been successful in communicating that pleasure.

Norman Arlott S.W.L.A.
Tilney St. Lawrence, Norfolk
1982.

Norman Arlott.

Gannet

SULA BASSANA

Little egret

EGRETTA GARZETTA

Little egret

EGRETTA GARZETTA

Norman Arlott

Louisiana heron

EGRETTA TRICOLOR

Norman Arlott.

White-faced tree duck

DENDROCYGNA VIDUATA

Norman Arlott

American wood duck

AIX SPONSA
ADULT MALE

American wood duck

AIX SPONSA
ADULT MALE

American kestrel

FALCO SPARVERIUS
ADULT MALE

Norman Arlott.

Black-winged stilt

HIMANTOPUS HIMANTOPUS

Norman Arlott

Little ringed plover

CHARADRIUS DUBIUS

Norman Arlott.

Barn owl

TYTO ALBA

Norman Arlott.

Turtle dove

STREPTOPELIA TURTUR

Norman Arlott

Kingfisher

ALCEDO ATTHIS

Norman Arlott

Grey-headed kingfisher

HALCYON LEUCOCEPHALA

Norman Arlott.

White-throated bee-eater

MEROPS ALBICOLLIS

Great spotted woodpecker

Great spotted woodpecker

DENDROCOPOS MAJOR
ADULT MALE

Norman Arlott.

Pied wagtail

MOTACILLA ALBA YARRELLII
ADULT MALE

Pied wagtail

MOTACILLA ALBA YARRELLII
ADULT MALE

Wren

TROGLODYTES TROGLODYTES

Wren

TROGLODYTES TROGLODYTES

Norman Arlott

Tufted tit

PARUS BICOLOR

Bearded reedling

Bearded reedling

PANURUS BIARMICUS
TWO ADULT MALES

Fairy-blue flycatcher

Fairy-blue flycatcher

ERANNORNIS LONGICAUDA

Norman Arlott.

Redstart

PHOENICURUS PHOENICURUS
ADULT MALE

Wheatear

OENANTHE OENANTHE
ADULT MALE

Scarlet-chested sunbird

NECTARINIA SENEGALENSIS
ADULT MALE

Ruby-crowned kinglet

REGULUS CALENDULA
ADULT MALE

Northern cardinal

CARDINALIS CARDINALIS
ADULT MALE

Bullfinch

PYRRHULA PYRRHULA
ADULT MALE

American goldfinch

CARDUELIS TRISTIS
TWO ADULT MALES AND AN ADULT FEMALE

Norman Arlott

Yellow-crowned bishop

EUPLECTES AFER
ADULT MALE

Norman Arlott

Blue jay

CYANOCITTA CRISTATA